Selfimprovement

Hello everyone.How are you doing today?I hope you are doing cool.
I am Johannes Mollo.I stay at Tembisa,in Gauteng.I am here to introduce you the book called Self Improvement.Now before we talk about this book,lets talk something else.
Ok.Let's talk about the purposes of individuals.Nowadays things are being more realistic.There is no doubt,no fear or what will people say if I do this and that.It has nothing to do with other people,of course,but what about the future,it does have something to do with it.Majority of people who are suffering today,is because either the decisions or things we just did without being aware that we are destroying our future.I am one of them.I call it mistakes.A mistake is not a death,or the end,is the beginning of knowing the right thing.That's why is good for us to learn to forgive each other,and also to learn from our mistakes,to accept the chances we are being given.This is what I wish I could do.I just hope is done by sharing it with you.
As I have told you about the book,it will help us reconcile,People will learn how to change,I couldn't go down with the topic because it would have made me create another book right here.

Self Improvement is a book that talks about how someone can overcome the failures that are caused by negativity and giving up instead of facing the challenges.It can help a lot,it provides light for people to discover hidden abilities and talents.It is also good for anyone who wants to see a change,or wishes to change the world,specially through rehabilitising people and helping people see the light.It consists of five chapters,of which most talk about taking control of your own mind,giving it your own prefered directions,making important decisions for life.Watch yourself turning your own life around by using the methods written in this book.Enjoy it.

Table of content

Chapters

Chapter 3

Chapter 4

Chapter 5

Summing it up

How to Make Your Attitude your Ally

In every aspect of your life, you attitude plays a big role. If you want to get ahead and be content in your life, then you have to make your attitude your ally.

Your attitude reflects in everything you do and everything that happens to you. What is referred to as The Law of Attraction is the concept that whatever you put out comes back to you. This is the whole idea of making your attitude your ally.

In order to make your attitude your ally, you have to learn what that means. You have to learn how to make your attitude positive and how to implement the idea of making your attitude your ally in your life.

It is going to take some work in order to be able to make your attitude your ally, but it is well worth it. As you will learn your attitude can paint your whole life and you can change everything about your current situation just by letting your attitude lead you.

What Does It Mean to Make Your Attitude Your Ally?

When you figuratively look at the idea of making your attitude your ally, what you see is that it, basically, means the attitude you display is going to reflect in the path you take in life. In other words, your attitude will affect your life and it will help in determining what happens to you.

Let us break it down and look at what 'make your attitude your ally' really means in simple terms.

First, you have to define what an ally is. An ally is basically a path you travel down. Your attitude is the way you act, think, and treat those around you. Your attitude affects everything in your life. It greatly affects the way you think and how others treat you.

Now to make your attitude your ally would mean to let your attitude guide you. Your attitude is going to shape everything in your life. You are going to be traveling down the path which your attitude leads you.

So, the best thing to do is to adapt a positive attitude so your ally is a positive path. You have to choose to adopt a positive attitude in order to make it your ally.

Making your attitude your ally is about choosing what that ally is going to be. Is it going to be negative or positive? Is it going to be about hard work or laziness? The attitude you choose to have in life is going to influence everything that happens during life, so choose that ally wisely.

It is a common understanding that your attitude shapes many aspects of your life. Many people believe that a positive attitude brings about positive things, while a negative attitude brings negativity.

A positive attitude has a way of even influencing your environment, but it may not be in the way you think. Just because you have this positive attitude does not mean that everything will automatically go your way.

When you think positively you will be less likely to see the negative in things and therefore your environment will appear to change. You will probably start to notice the little things more than ever before and that will have a nice effect on you.

You will be able to start believing in yourself. It will allow you to believe that you can accomplish something if you put your mind to it. You will be able to set goals and reach them because you will believe that you can do it. You will not have that negative energy to hold you back.

A positive attitude is very influential. It will start to shape everyone and everything around you. You are going to see the great power it has almost immediately. The power of a positive attitude is anything but subtle.

With this in mind, you have to decide what it is you want from life. Do you want positive things or negative things? That is really a silly question because most people are going to quickly say they want positive things, of course.

People can deal better with positive things than with negative things. People want to have a happy life without problems. They want that life that seems to just flow without road blocks and challenges around every corner. Of course, most people are going to choose a positive path for their life rather than a negative one.

In order to have good things happen you need to be very conscious to make your positive attitude your ally. You have to conduct yourself in positive ways, think about positive things, and live in a positive manner – you have to make your attitude your ally.

Ways to Make Your Attitude Your Ally

In order to get the influence of a positive attitude you have to first learn how to make your attitude your ally. How do you make your attitude your ally?

It is all about believing in the idea that your attitude affects your life and what happens to you. If you struggle with believing that if you think positive that positive things will happen, then the first step in making your attitude your ally is to change your way of thinking.

You have to believe in the idea that positive attitude equals positive results. You have to start looking for proof. It should not be hard to find, since positive influence is all around.

Try it out for yourself. There is no better proof than seeing it firsthand. Take one day and commit to having a positive attitude all day. Take notice of how others react to you.

Are they friendlier? Do people seem to help you out more than usual? What other things happen during the day? Can you see the positive attitude influencing other things in your life during the day?

Once you have convinced yourself that your positive attitude really does influence your life, then you can begin to put the idea of making your attitude your ally into play.

Keep up the positive attitude. Let it influence your life and let it lead you to good things. Eventually it will. You will start to see how it is bringing good things to you.

Making your attitude your ally should incorporate your ideas, the way you think, your actions and body language and even your goals.

You have to make an effort to start turning all your thoughts and ideas into positive thoughts and ideas. You have to start pushing the negativity out of your head and let positive thoughts guide you.

Every time you start to find your thoughts drifting to the negative, you have to make a conscious effort to make them positive instead. It helps to train yourself to always find the positive in anything. If you train your thoughts to go to the positive it will go a long way towards changing your attitude.

Your body language says a lot about you. Body language can tell others all about your attitude and personality. That is why it is incredibly important to make sure your body language is positive.

Body language is the movements of your body, the way you hold your body, and facial expressions, including eye movement. It often corresponds with our attitudes and sometimes contradicts what our words are saying.

When our body language and our words do not match, people are likely to believe the body language as it is often an unconscious thing that gives away the truth.

Positive body language is when your body is open. You do not want to do things that close your body off, like crossing your arms. You want to make eye contact and face people when talking to them.

A smile is the best body language you can display to others. Keeping a smile on your face will also benefit your attitude. Smiles have a way of making you feel good, so always be sure to have a smile on your face.

Goals are important in any aspect of your life. Goals can help you make things happen. Setting positive goals and sticking to them will help you maintain your positive attitude.

By maintaining your positive attitude and letting it lead you to good, you are making your attitude your ally.

Definition of a Positive Attitude

Just to put it out there in clear terms, here is a checklist of what a positive attitude is and what it involves.

Use this checklist to make sure your attitude is 100% positive. A positive person will have the following characteristics:

1. Upbeat and cheerful
2. Looks at the glass as half full not half empty
3. Can find the beauty in anything
4. Thinks of the good before the bad
5. Loves life
6. Avoids negative words
7. May seem silly at times
8. Loves to have fun
9. Never puts others down
10. Genuinely cares about those around him/her
11. Looks for ways to make others lives better
12. Is a giver, not a taker
13. Does not hurt others
14. Can see the solution over the problem
15. Willing to work towards goals

Do the things on this checklist seem like you or are they the opposite of how you act? If you really want to be a positive person, you will make yourself fit this checklist. You will strive to become everything here and to become a person that can honestly say this list describes them perfectly.

There are many ways you can begin to shape yourself into a positive person. Take some good tips to put to use in your life and help you become that positive person you strive to be.

Positive Living Tips

It is rather simple to separate the positive from the negative. However, it can be quite difficult to stop yourself from running to the negative. This is simple human nature. It is something we are programmed to do. Do not feel bad about this natural inclination. Instead, choose to do something about it.

Here are some tips for adding some positive influence to your life:

1. **Find a happy place.** Create a place in your mind that is your ideal paradise. When you feel stressed or down just go to your happy place, relax there and enjoy it.

2. **Get a hobby.** Doing something you enjoy and that will raise your spirits and allow you to maintain a positive attitude.

3. **Exercise.** While many people look at exercise in a negative way, it really can bring positive influences to your life. The body's reaction to exercise is a good one. You will feel better and therefore act better if you adopt an exercise routine.

4. **Find affirmations.** Affirmations are sayings, verses or other short pieces that have a positive influence. Affirmations can be a quote, a verse from the Bible or even a line from a greeting card. They are simply something that make you think positive or even just bring a smile to your face. Using an affirmation daily can perk up your attitude in an instant.

5. **Exploring new things.** Instead of walking away from the unknown, walk towards it.

6. **Do not walk away from a challenge.** Let yourself accept challenges and try creative ways to deal with them.

7. **Make a mess.** Make messes to learn. Do not get caught up in caring about the mess. Happiness can be messy and unrestricted.

8. **Ignore the rules.** You can end up having a fun time simply because you are doing something you were specifically told not to do. Defying authority can be an adrenaline rush. Break a few rules now and then.

9. **Pretend.** The imagination is a wonderful thing. Allow yourself to go to some make believe place. Get away for your normal life and pretend you are someone else. Have fun and you are sure to smile.

You can take these tips and build upon them. You can surely come up with things that have a way of making you happy. You know what makes you smile, so take that and run with it. Allow whatever it is that makes you happy to guide you to your new positive attitude.

Using Your Attitude As Your Ally

It may seem easy to just make your attitude your ally. You probably will not need a lot of convincing to at least give it a try. What do you have to lose? If you are used to letting your attitude lead you, then it is something you are already familiar with.

People make their attitude their ally all the time. Most of the time they do it without even realizing it. Unfortunately, most of the time the attitude is a negative one.

It is often easier to see how a negative attitude acts as an ally than how a positive attitude acts as an ally. This is just human nature to see negative over positive. We are more often drawn to drawing out the negative over the positive. Pessimistic attitudes seem to flood the world, while optimism is slowly drowning.

You can probably come up with many examples of how negative thinking or a negative attitude has turned into a negative situation. You can probably point out negative people and give plenty of examples how that negative attitude is influencing their life.

You may even be able to look at your own life and see how negativity has affected you. It's likely you have let a negative attitude direct you in at least one situation in your life.

Can you remember a time when your negative attitude caused problems in a situation? You can probably look at it now and see just how the negative attitude worked against you. Even if the situation was not a positive one to begin with, your negative attitude likely comes into play.

While this can teach you about how your attitude can become your ally, it also teaches you that you want to do everything possible to make sure your attitude is positive.

If you really want to make your attitude your ally and you want that ally to be positive, then you need to start looking at the positive. You have to train your mind to find the positive in everything.

You have to ignore the negative. Take the negative you can not ignore and turn it into a positive. Your ally does not need to be crowded with negativity.

Imagine your ally. An ally filled with negativity is crowded. There are road blocks and other things that get in your way or cause you to not be able to walk the path you choose. You may even have to work to get around these negative things.

If your ally is positive, then it is filled with positive things. There are no roadblocks that you can not handle. Anything that falls in your way is easy to get past. With an ally filled with positive things you will find that it is easy to travel and that you can get past anything that may come into your path.

You can clearly see that a positive attitude is much better than a negative attitude. You would, obviously, rather have an ally that is easy to get down, than one filled with things that get in your way and slow you down.

Using your attitude as your ally involves many levels of changing your life. You will have to change things you daily, through your interactions with other people, your thoughts and your goals.

As mentioned, the way you shape your thoughts and goals will go a long way towards helping you shape your attitude and making your attitude your ally. Make sure you make a conscious effort to keep these things positive.

When you interact with other people you are basically broadcasting your attitude. You want this to always be positive. People will react to you in a positive manner if you approach them in a positive manner. Your interaction with others is very important in your life.

You want those interactions to be positive. This will allow you to bring positive things into your life. A good example is during a job interview. If you approach the interview with a negative attitude then you likely will not get the job.

Go to the same interview with a positive attitude and you have a better chance of getting that job. The way you approach others can have a huge impact on your life, so make sure you are using your attitude as your ally when interacting with others.

Your attitude should be your ally everyday. It will take some time to make it routine. In the beginning, you will likely have to work hard to make sure you are being positive in every aspect of your life. You will have to make an effort to stay positive and to think positive. It can be difficult, especially if you often give in to negative thoughts and actions.

It is also common when you approach a situation in a positive manner that you end up having a positive experience. People are more likely to help you and to go out of their way to make sure you get what you need when you approach things in a positive manner. So with your attitude as your ally, you are opening yourself up to a lot of positive experiences.

Using your attitude as your ally is about making everything in your life positive. That means associating with positive people, keeping yourself in positive situations and surrounding yourself with positive things.

You have to get rid of negativity. You have to start being positive about everything. By doing this, you are creating your ally. You are paving your road with the positive and this will lead you to positive results.

What Making Your Attitude Your Ally Can Do For You

Once you start to live the idea of making your attitude your ally you will start to see changes, especially if you have been living with a negative attitude and have decided to change it to a positive attitude.

Adapting a positive attitude and making it the ally you travel through will impact your life in many ways. You are going to start to see the positive influence right away.

People are going to start treating you in a more positive manner. People respond positive to someone who greets them with a positive attitude. I am sure you have experienced this before. Think of a time when you gave a stranger a smile. They most likely smiled back, didn't they? That is a positive attitude at work.

It will not be that subtle either. You will be using your attitude to influence people in other ways, too. As you start to adapt your positive attitude to your life, you will begin to be able to see the positive in everything.

No matter what happens to you, your positive attitude will help you through it. You will find a way to overcome almost anything without getting mad, upset, or depressed about it. Basically, you will learn how to look at life differently.

You will be able to approach problems and difficult situations better. You will be able to handle adversity better. You will be able to overcome things that before would have dragged you down.

Making your attitude your ally may go even deeper than you could ever have imagined. If you suffer from an addiction, like smoking cigarettes, you may be able to quit once and for all just through making your attitude your ally.

Think about why you smoke. Many people give reasons such as they smoke to deal with stress, to calm them down, to relax. If you have a reason like this, then you will no longer need to smoke once you make your attitude your ally. This is because you will be able to handle stress on your own.

You will also be less likely to experience situations that you feel you can not handle. You will no longer reach for addictions, like cigarettes, to help you through stress because your attitude will be guiding you instead.

Quitting your smoking habit will become something that you will feel you can do because you will not feel that strong psychological need for a cigarette anymore. It is possible to help yourself through a hard habit, such as smoking, with your new positive attitude.

Making your attitude your ally will transform your life. You are going to be projecting a positive vibe and it will come back to you. You will start to see how positive things happen in your life. You will begin to draw positive influences to you. You will become a magnet for positive things. It will almost seem strange how much your new positive attitude affects your life.

You can look at making your attitude your ally in many different ways. It really depends upon your personal ideas and thoughts. Some people may believe that it is along the lines of karma and what you send out will come back to you. Others may believe it is simply a mental thing, where you think positive and therefore you see positive.

No matter what your opinion is on how a positive attitude works in your life, the bottom line is that making your attitude your ally is a winning idea. You cannot deny the power of making your attitude your ally once you start implementing it in your life.

A Constructive Example of Making Your Attitude Your Ally

It can be quite easy for someone to just tell you that making your attitude your ally is a good idea. However, until you actually see it at work, you may not fully believe in the idea. Here is a story about how making your attitude your ally can work beautifully. How it can help transform a lousy life into something great.

Janet was quite the pessimistic person. Janet approached every situation thinking the worst would happen. She never tried to even think positive. Janet rarely smiled and she often spoke negatively about everyone and everything in her life.

Janet had high blood pressure, no close friends, a job she hated and she was deep in debt. She read an article about how making your attitude your ally will help guide you in life and how that attitude needs to be positive if you want a happy and productive life.

Janet considered what she had read and decided to put the idea to work for her. She figured she had nothing to lose.

The next morning when she woke up, the same negative thoughts began creeping into her mind. Instead of embracing them as she usually did, she pushed them away and replaced them with positive thoughts.

Instead of anticipating the traffic jam she usually encountered on the way to work, she thought only about her favorite song playing on the radio and thought about how lucky she was to be able to hear that morning.

When she reached her office, instead of simply rushing to her office as she usually did, she smiled at a few co-workers and stopped to have a chat with the secretary.

Her boss even acknowledged her good work on the project she had just completed when he came in. She noted that if she had rushed to her office, she would not have even been standing there for him to talk to.

Later that day her boss called her into his office. He talked to her about how she seemed different today. He said he was glad to see her that morning because it reminded him of what a good worker she is and he realized she was perfect for the opening in management that he needed to fill.

Janet ended up getting a promotion.

After that day Janet kept making her attitude her ally. She trained herself to be positive and things started to really look up in her life. She made some friends at work and she started to feel better about herself and her life.

When Janet turned her attitude into a positive one and made her attitude her ally, she started to live a life she could only long for before.

The same thing could happen to you. Make your attitude your ally and see how it works out for you.

Why did this work for Janet? Take a constructive look at her situation.

Janet usually sat in traffic and fumed about how it was slowing her down. She went straight to the negative and even though her favorite song had probably played on the radio during her morning commute, she was so stuck in the negative that she never even heard it.

Today, Janet was open to hearing the song and when she did hear it she got a slight boost in the way she felt. It was that slight boost that helped her to remain calm and relaxed whole sitting in traffic.

Besides the immediate effect of Janet feeling more calm and being able to handle her traffic jam, there is also the fact that calming down and letting go of the stress is good for her health. Her blood pressure and pulse were likely lower than normal and that is great for her heart health.

Janet never greeted anyone in her office with any positive motions. She just went to her office every morning and sat by herself. Today, she actually took the time to smile at co workers and to even talk. She was able to start building relationships at the office which will help her to be happier about going to work and enjoy the office much more.

Having her boss come in while she was socializing gave her some much needed face time with him. Had she not been out there he would have never even considered her for the promotion.

Janet made many changes in her life just in one day. Imagine what could happen to you. Could making such a change impact your life in a big way too?

Yes it can. So you have nothing to lose by allowing yourself to try making your attitude your ally.

Summing It Up

Now that you have learned what making your attitude your ally means and how to implement the idea in your life, you can clearly see it is an idea worth putting to the test.

Through the ideas presented here you should be able to get started making your attitude your ally. You should find changing your attitude to a positive one is quite simple.

Once you put your mind to it, there is nothing stopping you from reaping the rewards of having a positive attitude and making it your ally.
It is all about taking that first step.

You have to decide to be committed to the process. You have to commit to becoming a positive person. You have to set a goal to become a positive person and let that positive attitude lead you.

Goals are very powerful. They can drive you and help you to accomplish things. When you have a set of goals you work harder and you feel as if you have to accomplish them. Set your goal to make you attitude positive and to make your new positive attitude your ally.

Remember what making your attitude your ally can do:

1 It can help you to look at life in a positive way.

2 It can allow you to see challenges and adversity in a new light that you are able to handle.

3 It can help reduce stress.

4 It can help you influence others to live in a positive manner.

5 It can make you a new person.

6 It can allow you to begin to love life.

Keep Janet's story in your mind and let it help you to stay committed towards your new positive attitude. Let the examples from her story remind you that good can come from all of this work.

You have learned what making your attitude ally means. You know that by projecting a positive attitude you will reap positive rewards. You learned what exactly a positive attitude is and how you can start to make your attitude positive.

You are armed with loads of information on how to become a positive person and how to live a positive life. The rest is in your hands. No one can force you into living positive. No one can make you make your attitude your ally. However, after all you've learned can you honestly say you would pass up the opportunity to make you life so much better?

Do you not want to see how great your life can be?

Are you sure you can live, knowing what you know now, without at least giving it a try?

Chances are you are now so excited about the possibilities that a positive attitude is all you'll think about over the next few days. Subconsciously you will start to change and by then, it will be too late to even consider ignoring all you've learned.

You will be on your way to making your attitude your ally without even putting up much effort. You will surely start to reap the rewards. But why wait? Making your attitude your ally is something that you can begin doing today, so what is holding you back?

Drop the negative thoughts. Put a smile on your face and start projecting your positive attitude to everyone. Take all the tips and advice you've read here and put it to use.

Make your attitude your ally. Change your life. Become a better person. Help those around you live a better life. Become a role model. Be everything you can be.

You have nothing to lose and everything to gain, so make your attitude positive. Then take your positive attitude and make your attitude your ally. Do it now and you will never want to go back to being a negative thinker again.

The Power of Positive Thinking

You have probably had someone tell you to think positive when you were in a trying situation. That is because the power of positive thinking is something that is a widely held belief.

Most people easily accept that when you give off positive energy, you can infect others with that positive energy and that they will return that energy to you. It is basically the idea that what you put out there will come back to you.

Positive influences are all around us. They exist because people love to feel good. People prefer the positive to the negative. You can likely relate to this. You would probably rather be around someone who is upbeat and full of energy than someone who is depressed and moping around.

People see that thinking positive and having a positive attitude can play a large role in their life. Positive thinking can be very powerful and by putting it to work in your life; you can reap the positive benefits.

What is Positive Thinking?

Positive thinking can be defined as thinking good thoughts or being optimistic. When it comes to positive thinking there is no room for the negative. When you are a positive thinker, you will always look on the good side of things. You will not dwell on bad things; instead, you will look for the good in them.

Positive thinking involves no negative thinking. Instead of thinking about what could go wrong, a positive thinker thinks about what can go right. A positive thinker is going to look for the good in things. That means they will always try to find something positive about every situation.

Positive thinking plays a large role in life. A person who thinks positive will end up having a more positive life then someone who thinks negative. A positive thinker is going to be able to stay upbeat in any situation. That is because they do not dwell on the negative. They can always find a way to look at the positive in any situation.

When bad things happen, a positive thinker is not going to let themselves get down and they are not going to let the bad invade their thoughts. Instead, they are going to look for positive things and look to find the solution to the negative situation.

They also adopt a different attitude than a negative thinker. A positive thinker is going to try to stay upbeat and happy. They are going to try to stay energized and not allow themselves to get down. If they feel tired or lazy, they are going to do something to help bring them back up.

Positive thinking can be used in every aspect of life, from the little things to major things. It can be used to help you get through trying times. You can also use it to just make your average day go a little better.

Positive thinking involves being able to see the good things, even in something bad. It involves being able to turn off the negative thoughts and replace them with good thoughts.

Positive thinking will allow you to avoid always going to the negative when something bad happens. It will also allow you to assume that good things will come your way and it will help you project an attitude that will help bring good things your way.

Positive thinking is something that allows you to turn negatives into positives. It allows you to look on the brighter side of life. Positive thinking will open your eyes and your life to a world that is brighter and better than the negative one most people dwell in.

Positive thinking will help you grow and be open to success. Through positive thinking, you will be able to allow yourself to start to envision your life as being positive and powerful. You will open up the door for good things to happen in your life.

Looking at it From a Child's View

Perhaps the greatest teacher of positive thinking is a child. Children are the ultimate positive thinkers. They have not learned that life throws curves and that challenges are around every corner. They look at life as a big adventure. Maybe you should adopt that way of thinking.

Think about a child in your life. They seem to have no fear of new things. They will try anything once. They love life and are optimistic and happy. Children love to explore the world and what life has to offer. They are willing to put themselves out there just to learn.

Children have to have this amazement for life. This is how they learn and how they develop their identity. It allows them to live in a positive manner.

Children do not jump to the negative because they believe there is good out there. They do not know about all the bad that the world holds because you shelter them from that.

Let yourself develop that child-like faith. Stop yourself from dwelling on the bad in life and start looking for the positive instead.

Think about that saying 'stop and smell the roses'. A child would do that, but would you? Chances are it is not likely you would. So, change that about yourself.

Slow down and take time to enjoy life. Stop filling everyday with to do's. Enjoy life and you will soon find it is easy to embrace the positive.

Here are some things that children do that you can bring into your life. These things will help you to be able to look at the positive instead of the negative.

1. **Explore new things**. Instead of walking away from the unknown, walk towards it. Children are always exploring. This is how they learn. Let yourself start exploring again.

2. **Do not walk away from a challenge**. When children are challenged, they get excited and look at it as a game. Let yourself accept challenges instead of walking away.

3. **Make a mess.** Children are messy. They love to make messes, but most of the time it is not just to make you mad. Children make messes because they are learning and they simply do not care if they get a little messy in the process. Happiness can be messy and unrestricted.

4. **Ignore the rules.** Children ignore the rules all the time. Often it gets them into trouble, but many times, they end up having a fun time simply because they are doing something they were specifically told not to do. Defying authority can be an adrenaline rush. Break a few rules now and then and let yourself feel like a kid again.

5. **Pretend.** Make believe is a big part of being a child. Almost everything you do revolve around pretending. The imagination is a wonderful thing. Allow yourself to go to some make believe place. Get away for your normal life and pretend you are someone else. Have fun and you are sure to smile.

There are plenty more ways you can use the influence of a child to drive your progress towards a positive attitude. You should watch children play. Just see what they do and take notes on how different their lives are from yours. How do they get through the day without stressing about every little thing?

Do not let yourself get hung up on the fact that they do not have responsibility. Responsibility should in no way hold you back from being positive. It is just an excuse and excuses kill the positive attitude you are working so hard to build.

Just focus on being child-like. Let yourself be free and just love life.

How is Positive Thinking Powerful?

Positive thinking is, obviously, something that can have a great impact on a person. What is hard to understand is why positive thinking is so powerful. That involves taking a good look at how positive thinking works.

Positive thinking works in three different ways. First, it works on you and your general attitude. Second, it works on those around you. Lastly, it has a way of influencing your environment. How exactly positive thinking works on these things is, open for debate, though.

Some people believe that positive thinking is related to karma. That whatever you put out there comes back to you. Others believe that positive thinking is a mental thing that triggers positive things. Whatever your beliefs, it is hard to doubt the power of positive thinking.

You will feel how powerful positive thinking is. Once you start to implement positive thinking in your life, you will start to see it work for you. Positive thinking has a way of changing your whole view on life. You will start to find the good in things and that will make you happy. You will be less likely to feel down and instead you will allow positive thinking to guide you to happy thoughts.

You will start to do everything in a more positive way, including how you treat others. This will not go unnoticed. Your interaction with others plays a large part in your life.

Other people are going to be greatly influenced by your positive thinking. You will start to see this because they are going to start treating you differently. Others will sense your positive attitude and they will treat you in a positive way. Someone who is often rude or just inattentive to you will likely start to treat you in a nice way or pay more attention to you.

You will start to find that people are more likely to offer you help when you need it. They will likely do nice things, such as hold doors open or just give you a smile. Your positive attitude may even be contagious. You may start to see people you spend a lot of time with exhibiting your positive attitude and positive thinking.

Positive thinking has a way of even influencing your environment, but it may not be in the way you think. Just because you think positive does not mean that everything will automatically go your way.

However, when you think positively you will be less likely to see the negative in things and therefore your environment will appear to change. You will probably start to notice the little things more than ever before and that will have a nice effect on you.

Positive thinking will allow you to believe in yourself. It will allow you to believe that you can accomplish something if you put your mind to it. You will be able to set goals and reach them because you will believe that you can do it. You will not have negative thoughts to hold you back.

Positive thinking is very influential. It is going to start to shape everyone and everything around you. You are going to see the great power it has almost immediately. The power of positive thinking is not subtle.

You have to make an effort to let positive thinking start turning all your thoughts and ideas into positive thoughts and ideas. It is up to you to start pushing the negativity out of your head and let positive thoughts guide you.

When you start to find your thoughts, drifting to the negative it is your responsibility to make an effort to make them positive instead. Go ahead and train yourself to always find the positive in anything. One you do this it will go a long way towards changing your attitude.

The power of positive thinking is that it will shape your life. Positivist is so contagious that it will affect the world around you. You will start to see positive thinking everywhere you go.

Positive thinking has a power that is undeniable. It is something that will not be subtle. It will have such a great impact on you and your life that you will wonder how you ever lived before putting it to work in your life.

The true power of positive thinking is that it allows you to live life to its fullest potential and for all that, it has to offer without letting negativity bring you down.

Positive Thinking and Body Language

Body language is something that we are not often aware of, but it sometimes can say more than our words ever could. That is why it is so important to pay attention to body language and always be aware of what it is saying to others.

Body language is the movements of your body, the way you hold your body, and facial expressions, including eye movement. It often corresponds with our attitudes and sometimes contradicts what our words are saying.

When our body language and our words do not match, people are likely to believe the body language as it is often an unconscious thing that gives away the truth.

When you are trying to implement positive thinking in your life, you also have to implement positive body language. When you are truly committed to a positive way of thinking then your body language will follow. However, if you are not whole-heartedly into positive thinking your body language could give you away.

It is very important that when you want to put positive thinking to work in your life that you become aware of your body language. You may actual want to learn a little about body language so that you can recognize negative body language and not let it interfere with your positive thinking and attitude.

A great example of how body language can affect others and reflect your inner feelings is the smile. It is likely that you have smiled at a stranger before.

What happened? Probably what happened is that they smiled back. Do you know that smile probably prompted them to smile at someone else and so on with your smile becoming contagious?

Smiles have a way of effecting people. One smile you give a stranger could prove to be just the motivation someone needs to be cheerful that day instead of grumpy. You never know.

Besides being contagious, a smile tells others you are happy. It says you are having a good day and you want to share that with them. A smile is powerful body language.

It is also common when you approach a situation in a cheerful manner with positive body language that you end up having a positive experience. People are more likely to help you and to go out of their way to make sure you get what you need when you approach things in a positive manner.

You should definitely learn about body language and make sure you avoid negative body language. It will take some effort at first until you train your body not use negative body language.

Body language can be a dead give away that your true feelings are not positive. That is why part of positive thinking involves positive body language.

Positive Thinking's Biggest Threat

You may believe, after reading this far, that negative thoughts are positive thinking’s biggest enemy, but that is wrong. As mentioned earlier positive thinking's biggest enemy is excuses.

When you make an excuse, you are opening a door for negative thoughts. Excuses are just your way of trying to trick your mind. You are trying to pass on responsibility for something every time you make an excuse.

Excuses can make becoming a positive thinker very difficult. If you are someone who is used to making excuses, then you will have a hard time becoming a positive thinker unless you stop making excuses.

Excuses are something that can make your mind think it is doing positive things when it really is not. An excuse will just make you think you are okay and not being negative at all, but in reality using an excuse is just a negative thought in disguise.

In order to be a positive thinker and put the power of positive thinking to work in your life, you have to get rid of the excuses. If you feel that you are about to make an excuse, then stop. Think about why you are making the excuse. What are you going to get from it? What benefit does this excuse have?

Try to identify what is really going on and why you feel you need to make the excuse. Are you just trying to sneak in a negative thought and trying to explain to your positive side why it is okay? This is common, especially when a person is just beginning to use the power of positive thinking.

Do not give up, though, if you start to find yourself making excuses. Just learn to be aware of this common tactic your brain has to try to keep the negative hanging around.

Putting the Power of Positive Thinking to Work

in Your Life

Many times people are drawn to the negative, so implementing positive thinking can be some work. You literally have to train your brain to think positive. You have to learn how to rid your mid of negative thoughts.

It may seem simple to think positive, but when you are used to thinking negatively, it can be quite difficult. You will be naturally inclined to go to the negative. You really have to make a conscious effort to fight off the negative and only stick with the positive. It can be a battle, but you can do it.

Ironically, by being a positive thinker, your issues with fighting off negative thoughts will actual be made easier. That is because your positive thoughts are going to be telling you that you can fight off the negative thoughts and that you can overcome them. You will have the necessary will power to stop negative thoughts in their tracks.

You will have to fully immerse yourself into positive thinking. You will have to surround yourself with positive influences. You have to be very focused on the positive and be committed to pushing away the negative.

Here are some things you can try to bring a positive spin to your life and make positive thinking easier:

1 **Read about positive thinking and positive things**. This includes reading books that are upbeat. You could also read inspirational things to help you get into the positive way of thinking.

2 **Use visualization.** You have to imagine yourself being positive, acting positive and thinking positive. You should picture positive things in your mind and allow yourself to think about positive situations.

3 **Use positive words.** Avoid negative words. Try to always make your conversations and thoughts positive. When you are thinking to yourself, use positive words. When you are talking to others, use positive words.

4 **Smile.** Use your smile to project your positive attitude. Let your smile speak for you. If you do nothing else, then put a smile on your face. It will do a world of wonder.

5. **Never allow yourself to quit.** A quitter's attitude is a big dose of negativity. Besides that if you quit, you will never succeed and failure makes it hard to keep positive. Additionally, quitting is associated with laziness and laziness is a symptom of negative thinking. When you think positive, you will not feel lazy or like you want to quit.

6. **Be aware of negative thoughts.** When you have a negative thought, you have to recognize it. You should figure out where it came from, why you are having it and how to deal with it. Being a positive thinker does not mean you can avoid all negative things. It means you learn how to constructively deal with them and not let them take you over.

7. **Be persistent with positive thinking.** You cannot let even one day go by without making sure you are thinking positive. You have to constantly be working on it until it becomes second nature.

8. **Identify fears that cause you to think negatively.** Often when a fear is confronted, it ends up being not as intimidating as it first seems. Fear is simply your lack of being able to see that bad things will not necessarily happen. When you learn to let go of fear and trust in yourself you will see it is easier to stay positive.

9. **Watch your emotions.** Try to stick to feelings of happiness, success and strength dominate you. Try to avoid feelings of weakness, fear and self-doubt.

10. **Do things that make you happy.** Watch happy movies, read happy books and listen to happy music. Surround yourself with happiness and you will begin to react to that.

11. **Hang out with other positive thinkers.** Try to avoid people who are often sad or unhappy. Avoid those who speak negatively or who act in a negative manner.

You have to make positive thinking your new lifestyle. It is just like changing your diet. Let's say you are giving up carbs. You are not going to tempt yourself with breads or really want to be around people who eat many carbs. The same can be said for positive thinking.

You are not going to tempt yourself with negative thoughts or want to be around people who are negative. You have to reshape your life so it fits your new style of thinking.

You may want to make sure that you are ready for such a change in your life. You should ask yourself if you are ready to be appositive thinker. Are you ready to let go of the negative? Are you ready to be optimistic? Can you really let go of the little things and look on the bright side of things? Are you willing to put forth the work that is necessary to become a positive thinker? You have to answer yes to these questions in order to truly be able to become a positive thinker.

It can help to set goals. Goals are very powerful. They can drive you and help you to accomplish things. When you have a set of goals, you work harder and you feel as if you have to accomplish them. You should set reasonable goals to help pave your way towards positive thinking.

Here is an example of some goals you can set:

1. Use a positive affirmation each day.
2. Try to complement someone everyday for a week.
3. Smile at everyone I see today

Through using goals, you can make your path to positive thinking much easier. You can watch your progress and be able to track how you are doing at implementing positive thinking in your life.

Becoming a positive thinker is something anyone can do. It is a matter of just putting your mind to it. It is going to be a lot of work, but it is well worth it.

The Impact of Positive Thinking

Positive thinking can have a huge impact in your life. It is the power of positive thinking.

Once you start to bring positive thinking into your life you are going to start seeing it at work. There is no doubt that you will begin to see rewards for all your hard work.

Positive thinking has a way of infecting everything in your life. You will begin by starting to wake up and go through your day feeling happy and upbeat. You will see the feelings of sadness start to fade away until eventually all you feel is happy, no matter what the current circumstances are in your life.

You will also see others start to treat your differently. You will begin to be greeted with positive words and actions. You will start to see your positive attitude become contagious and the people around you will begin to adopt your positive thinking.

You will begin to be able to handle situations better. When something bad happens, you will not fall apart, but rather look for something positive to focus on and help you through it. You will also be able to see the end of your troubles and that will make getting through it much easier.

You will begin to look at life in a different way. No longer will you fear the unknown, but you will embrace it and begin to actually enjoy learning new things and tackling challenges.

Positive thinking can do all of this for you. It can really reshape your life. It can help you live the life you have always wanted. You will be able to accomplish more and to reach goals that you once wondered if they were even possible. The impossible will become the possible.

It may seem crazy to believe that by simply changing the way you think can change your life, but it is true. Positive thinking can change your life because it has the power to do so. The power of positive thinking is strong and it works.

The Power of Positive Thinking at Work

It can be helpful to get an example of how something works in order to understand how it can work for you. Here is a story about John and how the power of positive thinking influenced his life.

John was in the middle of a very nasty divorce. His soon to be ex-wife was fighting him all the way about everything possible. He had trouble sleeping, eating and felt himself slipping into a great depression.

Every time he had to meet with his attorney, he experienced stomach pains and he was sure he was getting an ulcer. He was constantly worried about being able to make it after the divorce was finalized. He also worried about how this all was effecting his two children.

John was in a very bad place. Then, one day, he ran across some information about the power of positive thinking. He was so interested in what he read that he decided to see if it could work in his life.

John started to become aware of his thoughts. He started to push all the negative thoughts out of his mind.

Instead of approaching his situation with fear, he went towards it with courage. He stood his ground and did not give in. He laid down his demands and stuck to them. He stopped letting himself be walked all over by his ex.

John began thinking positively about his situation. He began envisioning a positive outcome. He stopped letting himself get down about what was happening in his life and started looking at all the positive things he had gotten out of it.

Now that he was separated, he felt happier. He could do whatever he wanted without having his wife nag him. He was closer than ever to his kids because he now cherished the limited time he was able to spend with them. He was able to get his financial affairs in order, too.

John was able to get through the divorce. He came out in the end without losing everything, being able to maintain a good relationship with his kids and even being able to somehow maintain a civil relationship with his ex.

By changing to a positive attitude, he was able to stop letting everything get him down. He was able to get through the trying situation without letting himself fall apart. In the end, the power of positive thinking was working for John, just as it can work for you.

You can see through John's story that positive thinking can get you through the rough times. It is not hard to believe that it can get you through everyday, too. Just as John changed his attitude and his way of thinking, so can you. You can make positive thinking work in your life and start turning your bad situations into good ones. You can get favorable results and outcomes, too.

Summing It Up

The power of positive thinking cannot be denied. Once you have seen it at work you will believe in it. Once you experience it you will wonder how you ever got by without it.

You have learned a lot about positive thinking and how powerful it is. You have learned how to define positive thinking, aspects of positive thinking and how exactly positive thinking works.

You have been given tips and advice to help you turn yourself into a positive thinker and how to use that new positive thinking power to change your life.

Positive thinking is a complete life change. It is more than just thinking with a can do attitude. Positive thinking is a life style and you have to adapt everything in your life to fit with your positive thinking life style.

You will see massive changes in yourself and those around you once you bring positive thinking into your life. The power of positive thinking is not a myth. It is true and real. You will see it if you begin to live with positive thinking.

The benefits are hard to deny. Once you start thinking positive you will begin to reap the rewards. It is not hard, either.

All it takes is some focused work to train your mind into positive thinking. With some work you will soon be able to put the power of positive thinking to work in your life.

Remember the story of John and how he used the power of positive thinking to get past a really tough time in his life. Also, keep in mind how excuses can work against you in your goal to become a positive thinker.

Innovative Thinking Secrets Exposed

Inventions and ideas are the products of innovative thinking. It is common for people to misunderstand innovative thinking. Inventors are often misunderstood, too. Innovative thinking is often looked at as being a waste of time, but nothing could be further from the truth.

It is common for an inventor to be looked at as being crazy or a bit 'off their rocker', especially if they have not invented anything that has hit the mainstream. Most of the world's famous inventors were once thought to be insane. That is until their inventions changed the world.

Inventors are a special group of people. They do not care what others think. They are all about their ideas and making something amazing that will help people or change the way of life. Without inventors we would be in a lot of trouble. It is inventions that have brought us things we use everyday, from toilet paper to computers. Inventions are important to our everyday existence.

What is Innovative Thinking?

Innovative thinking is thinking that goes beyond what you can see. It is imaginative. It is the ability to look beyond the obvious. It is creative and it is different. An innovative thinker can look at something ordinary and see the extraordinary.

Innovation is about invention. It is about being able to come up with something that nobody has come up with before. Being an innovative thinker means you have a mind that does not quite work like the logical, down-to-earth mind that the majority of people have.

Innovative thinking is a gift. Being able to go beyond the obvious is not something everyone can do. Some people are naturally born with this gift, while others have to work to train their brain to be able to think outside the box.

Innovative thinking is something that can help you out in many aspects of your life. You can use innovative thinking to create a new outfit, come up with a good business idea or create dinner.

Misunderstanding of Innovative Thinking

As mentioned, inventors and those who use innovative thinking are often looked at as strange. Most people do not see innovative thinking as being productive. However, it takes plenty of crazy ideas to produce one amazing idea.

Many people picture an inventor as someone who is scatter brained and not organized. They think of the quite, mismatched, clumsy inventor that is the stereotype for inventors. This is not entirely true and it does not have to be the image of innovative thinking.

Many times serious inventors are a bit scatter brained, but that is just because they are so focused on their work that they forget about everything else. It is not because they are crazy or insane. This is a huge misconception and it can be quite damaging because people do not want to become like this stereotype.

In general, people simply do not understand innovative thinking. One of the reasons for that is that people do not truly understand what innovative thinking is and how it can be productive.

Most people do not understand that innovative thinking is a skill. They do not see it as being a positive thing. Innovative thinking is actually a highly sought after skill in the business world. Being able to come up with new and useful ideas is something every industry can use.

Innovative thinking is often defined wrong. People think that innovative thinking has to be radical and way out there. That is not true. Innovative thinking can be simple or complex. It can be subtle, too. Innovation does not have to be a major change. Most people only recognize the radical innovative thinking, but it is important to recognize that not all innovative thinking is radical.

Another common misconception about innovative thinking is that it only involves new ideas. Actually, innovation is deeply rooted in using current ideas to bring about change. Many of the best inventions were taken from another idea.

Many inventors simply take an existing product and make it better through innovation. Innovation can also be taking ideas from other places and being able to put them together to create something new.

Innovative thinking is not just a quality of a brilliant genius. Many times people think there is no way they could be an innovative thinker because they are not 'smart' enough. Innovative thinking is not just a quality of those with high IQ's. The reason this misunderstanding exists is likely due to the fact that many of the great inventors were geniuses.

However, the genius mind simply makes them more open to new ideas and innovative thoughts. Anyone can be an innovative thinker. For some people, though, it just takes more work to learn the skill. You do not have to be a genius or have some fancy degree to invent the next best thing.

Innovative thinking is not a highly structured process. There are no rules to it. In fact, most innovation comes from clutter and disorganization. It is from the depths of many ideas and failed attempts that some of the greatest inventions of all time have been born.

You do not have to be highly organized to be innovative. It can help if you dislike chaos, but it is actually much easier to be innovative in the mist of chaos.

Maybe the idea of people yelling out ideas at random does not appeal to you. That is one of the best innovative ways to brainstorm, though. You do not want to limit your brain to certain hours it can be creative. Good ideas may come at the most horrible times. You have to be ready for them. You just can not expect the innovative process to be organized.

Listening to others may be of some assistance to innovative thinking, but in general, innovative thinking is the result of an individual. The famous inventors often worked alone and for good reason. Getting others involved can stall the innovative thinking process. Having too many distractions or having ideas thrown at you can interrupt your brains ability to think creatively.

Even though innovative thinking is often free flowing, it does not mean it has to be unrestricted. It is possible to get people together and have some structured innovative thinking sessions.

This is especially true in business. While you can not dictate when genius will hit, you can work in an environment that is very welcoming of innovation. It is possible to come up with amazing innovative ideas within the context of a business structure.

Many people believe the myth that innovation is expensive and has to involve technology. It is possible, even in today's high tech world, to have innovative ideas that do not require technology. Some of the best inventions involve no technology. They are simple and they work. You do not have to have a team of scientists and engineers at your disposal to bring innovative ideas to life.

Innovation is not perfect. Failure is a large part of innovation. Some people wrongly believe that there is no place for failure in innovation. That could not be further from the truth. Innovation is largely rooted in failure.

In fact, it is often failures that have led to some of the best ideas. Failure is actual a major part of innovation and something that can be learned from. Without failure there is no innovation.

Innovation is not an immediate gratification process. People who are looking for immediate rewards to their innovative thinking will be sadly disappointed. Many times people think that if they start working with innovative thinking that others will see them as being very smart and as being a go to person.

Unfortunately this just is not true. As mentioned, many times innovative thinkers have to earn their praise because people often look at them first as being a bit crazy.

Misunderstanding innovation can make it seem scary. The more you understand innovative thinking, the more likely you are to grasp the concept and be more likely to give it a try.

Skills that can Assist in Innovative Thinking

Innovative thinking is sometimes a God given gift. For most people, though, innovative thinking is something they have to learn. For the majority of people, learning how to be an innovative thinker can be a struggle. To make the process easier it can help for a person to recognize skills that can be helpful in innovative thinking.

Here is a list of skills you should work with to help you develop innovative thinking:

1. **Being able to look at something in a different way.** If you can look at a pencil, for example, and see it as something more than something to write with, then you are on your way to innovative thinking. Take that idea and run with it. While you may never come up with a great invention from it, you can use this brainstorming exercise to help develop your innovative thinking skills.

2. **Being able to look at what others have done and see a need for improvement.** If you can recognize things that are not quite perfect or that have the potential to be better, then you can be an innovative thinker.
3. **Being able to weed through piles of information to get to the good stuff.** If you can easily take a bunch of nonsense and make some sense out of it, then you can be an innovative thinker. You should recognize that innovative thinking involves a lot of nonsense and being able to get to the heart of things is a true innovative skill.

4. **Being committed.** Innovation requires a lot of commitment. If you are the type of person who can commit to something and who does not give up, then you are a prime candidate to be an innovative thinker.

You probably already have many skills of an innovative thinker. All you need to do is recognize that you have it in you. You can be an innovative thinker and use that ability to come up with many inventions and ideas.

How Innovative Thinking Works

Deriving new inventions and ideas form innovative thinking is a process. While thinking, in general, is usually not very well structured, there is a general structure that can help when working with innovative thinking. You have to have some path to follow so you can take something from an idea to an invention.

Innovative thinking starts with defining the situation. You have to look at what you are working with and define what is needed or what your desired outcome is to be. You basically have to know where you are going. Define what you want the final outcome to be.

Now you can gather information. Innovative thinking is not about just being able to come up with things out of thin air. You need to have background information. Find out what others may have already tried. By gathering information, you are able to avoid repeating others mistakes or you may possibly find an idea that you can work with to improve upon.

Next comes the actual innovative process. You are going to be brainstorming. You will be creative and inventive. Anything goes in this step of the process. There is really no room for logic. Sometimes innovation is born from an idea that seems unrealistic. A good example is cell phones. At one point people would have thought it was crazy to be able to walk around and talk on the phone no matter where you are. Today cell phones are a life staple.

After coming up with ideas you can then begin to go through them. Weed out those that are not going to work for one reason or another. Make a list of the most promising ideas. You are going to move on to work with these and develop them more.

Now you evaluate your list. You will try to develop these raw ideas further. At this point, you will likely see some emerge as being the most likely to work. You will also be able to get rid of a few more ideas.

You should now be able to define your final solution. You can begin to work on implementing the idea and making it a reality.

The process of innovative thinking is actually rather structured. You have some points where you can be unstructured and let your creativity take over, but overall you have to maintain some sense of structure so that your great ideas do not get lost or overlooked.

How to Use Innovative Thinking

It is one thing to decide that you would like to use innovative. It is completely different to actually start using it. It can be hard to decide how exactly to use innovative thinking to better yourself and the world around you.

It is most likely that you already have a job and are not looking to quit to become an inventor who wastes away your days trying to come up with the greatest idea of all times. That is not what innovative thinking is all about anyway.

You can use innovative thinking in your current situation. All you have to do is start working with your creative thoughts. Many times we simply push them away because our rational mind says they are not good enough or people would think we were crazy if we shared them.

Part of being an innovative thinker is not caring what others think. You have to be willing to put yourself out there and take criticism. You have to accept rejection will happen. Learn to take failure as a good thing. Learn from it and embrace it.

Here are some things you can do to help yourself become an innovative thinker:

1 **Ask questions.** Question everything. Be like a two year old child and ask why. You may even know the answer already, but ask anyway. Questions lead to ideas.

2 **Compare things**. Compare one thing to another and try to see what makes one better or more useful. Try to seek out things that are similar, yet different and figure out the best qualities of each and how you could put them together to make a unique product that has the best quality of each product.

3 **Think about what you want that you do not have now.** Imagine the future and think about where technology is going. Try to come up with ideas about things that would make life easier or better. Even if these ideas are not plausible right now, just let yourself imagine what if.

Things to Avoid when Trying to be an Innovative Thinker

Many things can get in your way when you are trying to be an innovative thinker. It is up to you to make sure nothing stands in the way of you and your great ideas. The following list is some things not to do when it comes to innovative thinking.

1. Do not let your rational mind hold you back.
2. Do not let others hold you back.
3. Do not listen to the negative.
4. Do not fear the unknown.
5. Do not be afraid of a great idea.
6. Do not censor yourself.
7. Do not ignore ideas.

As you can see many times you are the main road block to innovative thinking. It can be your own thoughts and feelings that do not allow your innovative ideas to flow. You have to be responsible for making sure that you allow your mind to be creative and to think outside the box.

Things to do to Help you Be an Innovative Thinker

Just as there are things not to do, there are some things you should do to help you on your path to innovative thinking. The following list explains some of these things to do.

1. Do allow yourself to get silly.
2. Do let your mind wander.
3. Do question everything.
4. Do try new things.
5. Do let your inner child take over.

These things you can do are actually quite simple. Really al they involve is stopping your natural instincts to be grown up and act in a mature manner all the time. Sometimes, though, it is fine to let the immature side of yourself come out, especially when it comes to innovative thinking.

Some Exercises in Innovative Thinking

Becoming an innovative thinker is actually a fun process. You are going to be able to let yourself let go and think freely and creatively. You will be able to ignore all the rules of logic and just think whatever and however you want.

Deriving ideas and inventions from innovative thinking involves first getting your brain on board with the task. In order to do that you will need to do some exercises in innovative thinking.

These exercises can help you to get your mind thinking in an innovative way rather then as do on a regular daily basis.

Exercise 1: **Day dreaming.** We have all, at some point in our life, day dreamed. It should not be too hard for you to come up with a day dream. Everyone wishes they could fulfill their goals and live their dreams, so go ahead and do it. Just take some time to relax and day dream about a life you wish you had or day dream about somewhere you would like to go.

If you really want to be creative record your day dreaming and talk about what you are seeing. This will allow you to go back and remember the day dreaming exercise. You may even be able to get some ideas form it later on.

Day dreaming just allows your mind to forget the reasonable and forget the average day to day life. It allows you to imagine and think about the possibilities.

Exercise 2: **Free write.** Free writing is where you just sit down with a blank sheet of paper and write whatever comes into your mind. You do not worry about grammar or anything. You just put the words on the page as they enter your mind.

When you first try free writing you will likely see that your logical thinking is hard to turn off. You may write about nothing creative at all. That is fine. As you get into the exercise you will be able to come up with more creative things. It is not about creating a story or making any sense. It is about learning how your mind works.

When you are finished with your free writing exercise, read over what you wrote. Look for anything that you could expand upon. If you have some good ideas, then take them out and consider free writing on that particular topic.

Exercise 3: **Play with clay.** This is similar to free writing. Instead, though, you are going to be shaping and molding a piece of clay. Just let yourself get lost in the clay. Look at its color, feel its texture, smell its smell. Let yourself mold it and shape it however you are led to do.

This is a great way to distress. Playing with clay is relaxing and it is something you can do easily. It does not require any thinking at all, actually. It allows your mind to turn off and rest, which is great when you are trying to work it hard to be innovative.

Exercise 4: **Spend a day with children.** Children are the best innovative thinkers. As we grown up we tend to lose that wonder and amazement for life that drives innovative thinking. Spending a day with children can help you get back to that mind set and allow yourself to open your mind to innovative thoughts.

Children will give you so many ideas and they will bring out the child in you. Spending time with them will allow you to remember what you were like at that age. You will be quicker to be able to remember how you looked at the world and how full of wonder you were.

Exercise 5: **Do something new.** You can try something you have never done before or try something that scares you to death. Trying something new opens you to new experiences where you can learn a lot about yourself and the world around you.

Doing something new can even involve just learning about a different part of the world or it could be as dramatic as jumping out of a plane. Do whatever your mind leads you to.

Doing something new will stimulate your brain in many ways. You will be full of excitement and you will be learning at the same time. You will stimulate your brain to release triggers that can help spark creativity.

Exercise 6: **Learn a musical instrument.** Playing music allows your brain to use the part of it that is responsible for creativity. This will open up the ability for your mind to go ore easily into the mode needed for innovative thinking.

You can learn an instrument or even try out singing. Just do something that will stimulate the creative sections of your brain and help get them warmed up so you can begin thinking creatively.

These exercises can do a lot to help you learn how to be an innovative thinking. You can try them all or only a few. It is up to you. Let yourself try out fun things, like these exercises. Make time to do things like this. You have to do things like these exercises in order to allow yourself to learn to be a creative and innovative thinker.

Innovative Thinking and Passion

One thing that has not been mentioned yet is about the role passion plays in innovative thinking. It is true thought. You have to have passion about your innovative ideas or you will never get anywhere with them.

You have to feel strongly that your ideas are worthy. You have to believe in yourself and know that your ideas are good. IF you do not stand behind your ideas, then it will be quite hard to get others on board with them.

Being passionate about innovative ideas is not something that you can learn. It is something that comes from the heart. It is something that is uncontrollable.

You have to be able to tell others about your innovative idea and get them excited. It is impossible to do that if you do not have any passion about your product.

It is hard to develop passion.

However, if you immediately feel very strongly about an idea you come up with, then chances are it is something worth going with. When you have that immediate passion about something then it is natural and it really is something you believe in.

It is your job to make sure people know about your passion for your idea. It is hard to argue with someone or put down their idea if they seem so passionate about it. Let people know that you really do care about your idea and that you will not be quick to let them push it aside.

Persistence and passion go together when it comes to inventions and ideas. People are quick to ignore or put off things that are new. People will likely not be nearly as interested in your idea as you are, so you have to be ready for that.

You have to keep pushing your idea in front of people. It is the passion that will drive you to do this. So never let go of the passion. Never allow yourself to lose your fight and drive. Always stand behind your idea. Always know what to say – be prepared.

When people come at you with negative remarks or even questions, then you have to be available to answer back. You need to know the ins and outs of your idea and you have to be able to explain every detail so you can talk to others about it.

Do not forget about passion when it comes to innovative thinking. If you forget the passion then you will likely end up never getting your idea recognized for the brilliance they are.

An Innovative Thinking Story

Here is a story about Sue. Sue is an innovative thinker. She has not always been, though. Sue found her innovative genius one day and has never let it go because of what it has done for her in her life.

Sue is an average woman. She has no extraordinary talents. She is not a genius. In fact, Sue never even went to college. What makes Sue different is that Sue is a great innovative thinker.

The company Sue works is for a big name company that usually only hires in the best of the best. Her co-workers all have degrees from top universities. They were valedictorians and honor students. Sue does not feel out of place, though, because she knows she often produces work that they could only dream of producing. That is all because of her innovative thinking.

Sue was not born an innovative thinker. She had to work at it. It took her many years to perfect the art of innovative thinking. She had to do many exercises and had many failures.

Sue would spend a lot of her free time free writing and brainstorming. She also started to look at the world around her. She started to question everything. She started to look at everyday things and wonder how she could make them better.

One day she had a break through and came up with an idea that changed her life forever. Sue invented a product that became very popular. She was recognized on national television and she started getting phone calls form various companies who wanted her on their team.

Sue ended up at her current job and she has never been happier. Her innovative thinking has led her to a life she could only dream of before.

Innovative thinking is amazing. It can work wonders in your life. All it takes is just getting started. You can make it work for you. You can build upon your innovative ideas and create something wonderful. You can use innovative thinking to make you stand out from the crowd.

Be like Sue and make your own future. Go out there and create, imagine and invent. Use innovative thinking to guide you to the future you have only dreamed about.

Summing It Up

You now know all about innovative thinking. By now you have probably changed how you see innovation. You now know how powerful it is and how it can work in your life.

You know the definition of innovative thinking. You also know about the common misunderstandings and how they can turn people off on innovative thinking. This knowledge can really help push you towards wanting to be an innovative thinker because you can see just how much it can do for you.

You have learned the exercises and the techniques that will help you to become an innovative thinker.

You know innovative thinking is not just for inventors or geniuses. You know everything you could possible want to know about innovative thinking.

To sum it up you have to understand that innovative thinking is:

1. Powerful.
2. Passionate.
3. Creative.
4. Amazing.
5. A skill.

Innovative thinking is so powerful that it can change the way people look at you. It can change the world around you and it can change you. You can use innovative thinking in every aspect of your life.

Innovative thinking is about passion. You have to dig deep to be able to stand behind your new and unfamiliar ideas. You need that passion to make others see just how great your idea is and the possibilities that it holds.

Innovative thinking is all about creativity. It is constructive, but at the same time it is free and it flows. You are not restricted, except by your own mind. You can do anything when you are an innovative thinker because you learn not to hold yourself back and to explore the world and let your experience new things.

Innovative thinking is amazing. Innovative thinking is responsible for many of the greatest inventions in the world. Innovative thinking is responsible for making our lives as they are today. The modern conveniences that we could not imagine living without are al part of innovative thinking.

Above all, innovative thinking is a skill. You do not have to be born with it. You can learn to be an innovative thinker. You just have to put your mind to it and work at it. You have the ability to train your brain to be innovative.

Everything you have read about innovative thinking sums it up nicely. You know about every aspect of innovative thinking. You know how it works, how to develop the skill yourself and how to use it.

You should keep the do's and don'ts in mind so you can help yourself in any way possible. It may be easy to say do this and don not do that, but it is a fact that there are some things you have to do in order to allow yourself to be an innovative thinker.

You hold the key to becoming an innovative thinker. You hold the key to allowing your mind to be something great.

You can begin to put innovative thinking to work in your life if you only put your mind to it. If you struggle with letting your mind be innovative, then remember the story of Sue. Remember how she managed to push her rational thoughts aside and let innovative thinking lead her to success.

You can change the way you think and that can change your life. Put innovative thinking to the test. Let your mind wander and let it do something great.

You do not have to become a famous inventor. You do not have to become scatter brained and focus so much on your ideas that you do nothing else in life. Innovative thinking can co-exist with your regular life. So do not be afraid just get to it!

erything in your mind that you have learned so that you are ready to become a positive thinker and to be able to really benefit form the power of positive thinking.

Do not walk away from reading this and forget what you have learned. There are some valuable lessons, from learning to think like a child to how to stop negative thoughts. This information is going to be the backbone of your quest to positive thinking.Do not let yourself live without giving the power of positive thinking a try. It is well worth the work. You can be a positive thinker and you can change your life through the power of positive thinking.

How to Adopt Creative Thinking

Creative thinking is the ability to let your mind create thoughts that are often different and unusual. Creative thinking evolves around the idea of thinking beyond the scope of the norm. It is all about being able to think outside the box and be original in your thought process.

Creative thinking is something you can train your mind to do. Some people are actually born with creative thinking abilities, while others have to really work to let themselves be a creative thinker. However, it is possible for anyone to become a great creative thinker whether they were naturally born or they have to work at it.

You hold the key to adopting creative thinking in your life and by doing so; you could change your life, your thoughts and your world, forever.

What is Creative Thinking?

Have you ever had an amazing idea that just seems to be the ideal solution to a problem? Has anyone ever told you that you are amazing when you have shared an idea? Have you ever solved a problem that nobody else could solve? If you answered "yes" to any of these questions, then chances are you already know what creative thinking is.

Thinking, in general, is a process. It is natural. We all do it and it usually is not something we spend a lot of time perfecting. However, in some cases, the ability to be a creative thinker is important.

Creative thinking is all about being able to come up with ideas and thoughts that are not something the average person would come up with. Creative thinking can be defined as thinking outside the box, which means thinking beyond the normal scope.

A good example of creative thinking is coming up for different ideas of how to use a common product. The common product already has an identifiable use or uses. However, there are also probably other ways the product can be used. Creative thinking would help a person to define other ways to get use form the common product.

Creative thinking can involve many techniques. It takes some certain skills to be a creative thinker, too. Creative thinking is usually something people have to work to gain it because it is not usually a second nature.

When a person develops their creative thinking abilities, they will find they can come up with ideas quickly. They will likely find that they think differently then others and come up with ideas that are not at all like others. They will likely begin with the not-so-obvious answers to questions instead of jumping right in with the obvious solutions.

A creative thinker is someone great to have around because they will be able to give multiple ideas at a time. They will not give up easily and they will be a great contributor to a problem-solving situation.

What are the Benefits of Creative Thinking?

Creative thinking has numerous benefits. It is a great skill that can really boost your value in the business world. Being able to think creatively can be a huge benefit to almost any industry or business.

Creative thinking allows a person to come up with multiple ideas rather quickly. Once a person is a skilled creative thinker, they will be able to just come up with ideas in the blink of the eye. Being able to think quickly can help in professions where time is of the essence.

Creative thinking can make a person a perfect problem solver. Being able to think creatively allows a person to come up with solutions to problems that others may never even think about. A person is able to come up with good ideas that may not be so obvious. Creative thinking is something that can be a huge benefit to almost any profession because quick thinking is a great skill.

Creative thinking can give a person a completely new outlook. They will be able to use it in their professional and personal life. They will start to implement creative thinking techniques no matter what they are doing because it will come naturally.

Creative thinking can change a person whole attitude. It will make them more confident and allow them to live up to their full potential because they will not doubt their abilities. It can be a real moral booster and allow a person to really show what they can do.

Above all, creative thinking can be a ticket to success and great accomplishment. A creative thinker is hard to hold back. They are always thinking and they are always on top of their game. It is hard to deny a creative thinker anything because they are good at what they do. They are able to bring their creative thinking to the table to help improve their life and accomplish their goals.

Creative thinking has some amazing benefits. It is hard to deny that creative thinking can do a lot for a person. It is easy to start being a creative thinker and make it change your life.

How Can I Adopt Creative Thinking?

You probably are very interested by now in how you can adopt a creative thinking mindset. It will take some work to train yourself to use creative thought, but it is actually quite a fun process. You get to be creative, silly and allow yourself to go into the world of fantasy.

Good thoughts are not necessarily the most rational thoughts. Think about it. Many of the inventions we use today were once thought to be crazy ideas. That is what makes creative thoughts so great. Nobody else is likely to think of them, but once they hear them they wish they did.

One of the things you can do to become a creative thinker is called "thought experiments". Thought experiments were actually used by Albert Einstein. Albert Einstein is said to be one of the greatest thinkers of all times. He used these thought experiments to stimulate his mind and help himself to see beyond the obvious and get creative.

A thought experiment is basically a way to allow your mind to go places you might not normally let it go. It allows you to use all aspects of your thinking ability. It opens up doors in your mind that may never have been open before.

Thought experiments are simply rooted in your mind. They are not physical and therefore do not have to be plausible. You can do anything you want with a thought experiment. They allow you to explore the world around you.

The basics of a thought experiment involve visualization. Visualization is merely forming an imagination in your mind or following through actions in your mind through picturing them. Being able to visualize something is a large part of creative thinking.

Thought experiments involve a few other things then just visualization. The following list covers other things you will need to do to create thought experiments.

1 **Develop deep thought evoking questions that you want to find the answers**. These questions can be questions that can be answered or rhetorical questions. They can even be universal questions to which the definitive answer could never be determined.

2 **Think about great geniuses**. Imagine yourself sitting down and having a deep conversation with this genius. Imagine what you would ask and how they would answer.

3 **Imagine traveling in time or to another dimension.** Imagine what it is like. How does it look? What are the people like? Are there even people? Create every aspect of life.

4 **Think about God or whatever higher being you believe in.** Think about the questions you would ask and his answers. Try to imagine being in the presence of such power.

5 **Experiment with astral projection.** Get a book and study up on the idea. Then try it.

Try to float out of your conscious body and into the astral plain.

Another great thing to do to stimulate creative thinking is asking 'what if' questions. Develop a list of things you would like to know. Try to answer a 'what if' question in many different ways. See how creative you can be. Go in detail with your answers and get really deep into answering what if something happened.

There are plenty of ways to become a creative thinker and to help your brain to think creatively. Here is a list of some additional things you can do to help make yourself more creative in your thinking process:

1. **Learn to use breathing to relax.** By being able to regulate your breathing and focus deeply on it, you can clear your mind and allow creative thoughts to flow more freely.

2. **Practice visualizing things.** If you have problems with visualization, then start out small with visualizing simple things in your head and then moving onto things that are more complex.

3. **Gather information on things you are interested.** This will help give you something to think about. You can think about how to build upon what already exists and how your creative thinking can change it or make it better.

4. **Find a friend to brainstorm with.** Getting someone else in on your creative thinking means you can work together. Having someone else's perspective on things can really get the creative juices flowing.

5. **Try thinking as if you are someone else.** Sometimes we get stuck in our own mindset. Creative thinking is about going beyond our comfort zone and thinking outside the box, so pretend you are someone else and think how he or she would think.

6. **Challenge your brain often.** Give your brain a workout by doing puzzles and trying new things. This will expose you to different ideas and you can add that to your mind bank of ideas.

Some Creative Thinking Examples

You may not know where to begin with your thought experiments or using 'what if' techniques.

The list below offers some great examples of creative thinking exercises that you can try. These exercises work to help you expand your thinking from being narrow to being able to look at a full range of ideas.

1 **Imagine yourself living on the moon.** Picture what it looks like. Take yourself through a whole day. Think of every little detail, like where does water come from? How do you breathe? Are there other life forms? What do you eat? How do you travel? What is your home like? Are you alone there or are there other people? How did you get to the moon? Who owns the moon?

2 **Imagine yourself living a whole day as an animal.** Think how that animal must think. Think about interacting with other animals. How do you feel? What do you eat? Do you talk with other animals in your own language or how do you communicate? Where do you live? Do you have a family? Do you work? What activities do you do? Is there a form of government or some type of animal that is in control?

3 **Write a description of the room you are in.** Give details about every little thing, from the books on the shelf to the tiny crack running along the left corner of the room. Make sure you are very detailed, so detailed that someone reading it would be able to completely visualize the room. You want to give descriptions that reach all five senses. Use colors, smells, textures along with your visual descriptions.

Your thought exercises should well beyond rational thought. The whole idea is to challenge your mind and get it to have to be creative. You want your mind to have to work to come up with answers.

You can create your own thought experiments. Be creative in coming up with them. The process of creating thought experiments is, in itself, a way to stimulate creative thinking.

Some 'what if' ideas that you can use:
What if ---

1 I lived to be 200 years old?
2 I was born a different race or gender?
3 I lived somewhere else in the world?
4 I had not gone to college or had gone to college?
5 The world was flat?
6 I did/did not have children?
7 There was world peace?

8 Einstein was never born?
9 Animals could talk?
10 I could spend one day with God?

By looking at these examples you can probably now better come up with some of your own. You can feel free to use these examples, too. Just make sure your questions are challenging and something you will really have to think about.

Another thing you can do to help your creative thought is ponder age-old questions or rhetorical questions. Think about things like:

1 God
2 Creation/Evolution
3 Fate/Destiny
4 Coincidence

Here are some common questions that people often ponder that you can use to get your creative mind working:

1 Is there life after death?
2 Is there really a God?
3 Did Adam and Eve have belly buttons?
4 Which came first – the chicken or the egg?
5 If a tree falls in the forest, does it make a sound?
6 Would an orange be called an orange if it was green?
7 Why isn't a banana called a yellow or an apple called a red?

You can also challenge your brain by trying to solve old cold cases. If law interests you this may be a perfect idea for you to explore. Find a cold case and see if you can solve it. Besides just stimulating your creative thinking, you may also end up helping someone.

There are so many ways you can stimulate your mind to think creatively. Just allow yourself to think freely and try to find ways to challenge your brain.

What Skills Help in Creative Thinking?

If creative thinking does not come naturally to you then do not worry, you can still develop the skill. You do not have to be a natural. In fact, all you need is to bring the skills you have to the table and build upon them to make yourself a creative thinker.

Here are some skills you likely have already that can be used to develop creative thinking:

1 **Organizational Skills** - Being organized may seem the opposite of being creative. When people think of creativity they often thin unstructured thought and unorganized behaviors, but actually creative thought can be quite organized. When you are organized, you are able to better sift through your thoughts and get to the heart of the good idea.

2 **Reasoning Skills** - Being able to reason is very helpful in creative thinking. Reasoning skills come in handy when you are analyzing a situation. You are able to decide right away what will work and what will not work.

3 **Objectivity** - Being able to be objective allows you to consider many possibilities and not just be stuck on the obvious. This is key to creative thinking.

4 **Any skill in the arts** - This includes music, writing and artwork, like painting or sculpting. Having these artistic skills means your mind is already used to thinking outside the box. You have the ability to be creative and therefore you are predisposed to creative thinking.

While creative thinking is a skill itself, it does take other skills to be a good creative thinker. You may already have the skills described above or if you do not, then it can help to develop those skills before you start to work on creative thinking skills. This will help you to make developing creative thinking a little easier.

Creative Thinking Techniques

The way a person goes about creative thinking is a very individual process. There really are no hard-set rules, but creative thinking, as any way of thinking, usually follows a general process. Understanding the general process can help you to be a better creative thinker and make it easier for you to be a creative thinker.

The creative thinking process involves four steps.

Step 1: Analysis
You begin by looking over the situation. You should take in everything you can about the situation. Get details and ask questions. You must really get to know the situation at this point.

Analysis involves finding out the who, what, where, when and how of the situation. Once analysis is complete, you should be able to completely explain the situation including any obvious problems or issues.

Step 2: Brainstorming
This is the true area of creative thinking. Once you know about the situation, you can begin to start thinking. You can brainstorm in any manner that works for you. You may just shout out ideas or may write them down. Whatever works for you is best to do.

Brainstorming can take on many forms. You can write things down, talk things out or even conduct experiments. Brainstorming should be free flowing and recorded so no good ideas are lost.

Step 3: Break It Down
Now that you have a nice collection of ideas, you can start going through them and weeding out ones that will not work. You may find that if you change an idea just a little that it will work much better. This step is all about tweaking your ideas.

You will go over all of your ideas and weed out those that are not going to work. You should end up wit h the ideas that seem to be the best solutions.

Step 4: Review
The final step involves getting your final idea. This will help you to come up with one or two ideas that seem to stand out and be the best ideas.

You will go over the ideas you have left and narrow them down even more to one or two plausible ideas. You should then be able to go into detail of how each idea will work and how it will be implemented.

Being a creative thinker involves being able to think without a lot of structure, but these four steps are the basics of any thinking process. They may help you to be a better creative thinker.

How to Become a Creative Thinker

So you want to be a creative thinker? You have decided that you love the idea of being able to come up with amazing ideas at the drop of a hat. Well, then it is time to learn how to become a creative thinker.

Becoming a creative thinker is about training your mind and making a conscious effort to be more creative. Start out by letting yourself be more creative in general.

As mentioned before, skills in music and the arts can go a long way towards helping you to become a creative thinker. You may consider taking up an artistic hobby to help get your creative juices flowing.

The reason that these skills help so much with creative thinking is because they open up the creative areas of the brain. They allow a person to let go of their rational thoughts and free the brain up for more creativity. The more you can allow your brain to be creative, the more likely you will be able to draw upon that creativity at will.

You can also just sit around and brainstorm ideas. See what you can come up with. Get out a pen and paper. Just write down whatever comes to mind. Do not censor yourself. Let your thoughts flow freely. You will likely be amazed at what you end up writing when you go back and read it.

Try the thought experiments and 'what if' ideas given earlier. Do at least one of these daily to keep your mind sharp and your creative juices flowing. Take them seriously and be committed to doing them.

You have to put forth some effort to try and get your brain into the habit of creative thinking. It involves commitment. It involves daily work. You cannot slack at all if you truly want to develop a brain that can think creatively.

Adopting creative thinking is something anyone can do. You just have to be able to let your mind wander and stop being so in control of your ideas. Creative thinking is free flowing.

You have to practice often. Let your mind just go beyond the obvious and see what you can come up with. Try some things like free writing where you let your thoughts be control. Play games that get you thinking and that will get your brain working. Challenge yourself. Try something new.

You know what is creative, so just let yourself get into creative activities. Anything that will allow you to go beyond your normal boundaries is going to stimulate creative thinking. You have to be willing to go outside your comfort zone and start to experience things you have never experienced before.

Becoming a creative thinker is a matter of just putting your mind to it. Once you decide to be a creative thinker, nothing is holding you back but yourself.

A Lesson in Creative Thinking

Creative thinking can be a very beneficial skill in business. Take the following story about Ryan and Scott as a good example of how creative thinking can get you ahead at your job.

While reading this story try to consider yourself in this situation. Think about who you are more like and who you want to be more like.

Ryan always thought he had it in good at work. He worked for a great company where he was always praised for his hard work. Ryan held a business degree from a notable school and thought he had learned everything he needed to already.

One day there was a new employee who joined the team at work. He worked in the same department as Ryan and he held the same position in the company as Ryan. This new guy, Scott, was rumored to be some sort of genius.

Ryan wondered what was so great about Scott. He had talked with him and learned he had graduated with a business degree form some state college and that this was his first position after graduation. Ryan did not see anything special.

At the weekly meeting, the boss told the employees that there was a client who would be coming in later in the week to hold a meeting and decide if this was the company they would like to do business with. He needed a presentation prepared to present to the client by Friday. He asked that everyone brainstorm some ideas and later that afternoon they would meet again to go over them and choose the best idea.

At the afternoon meeting, there were plenty of mediocre ideas tossed around. When Ryan's turn came, he felt pretty good. He proposed a nice idea that was a little different from the other that had been presented. His boss commented that so far it was the best he heard.

Then it came Scott's turn to present his idea. Scott blew everyone away with his amazing idea. He had a creative approach to the presentation that would really make it something different. He had almost come up with the complete plan. There would be little work to do to make it ready for Friday's client meeting. The boss was so proud he decided to let Scott make the presentation himself.

Ryan could not understand how Scott came up with such an idea in the short amount of time they had. After the meeting, he talked with Scott. Scott explained that he used creative thinking to help him. He told Ryan all about how creative thinking works and how it had helped him land this job in the first place.

Ryan was amazed and he decided to give creative thinking a try himself. He started reading about creative thinking techniques. He even spent some time everyday asking himself 'what if' questions and trying out thought experiments.

Soon Ryan and Scott became the two top employees in the office. They were using their creative thinking to climb the corporate ladder. They ended up working so great together that eventually they started their own company and within a year, it had a net worth of over a million dollars.

Creative thinking had transformed Scott's whole life He was living the American dream. He would probably never have gotten there without the help of a little creative thinking.

Ryan's story is probably much like yours. Until you actually learned about creative thinking, you probably never gave the idea a second thought. You may not have even realized what a major skill it is.

It is amazing to think that creative thinking can help someone land a good job and get recognized for their work on their very first day, but it can happen. Think about Scott when you are at work. Is there someone in your office who seems to be like him? Are you like him or are you more like Ryan? Skills are what will help you advance at work, not your degree.

Book smarts can only take you so far. You have to really get your brain working in order to make a big impact on your boss. Creative thinking is the way to do that.

Put creative thinking to work for you. You could end up being the star of the office, just like Scott.

Summing It Up

Creative thinking can help you to do many things. It can help you get ahead at work, learn new things and explore the world in ways you had never done before. Creative thinking can offer you so much. You can get so many benefits form creative thinking it would be a shame if you did not grasp the concept now that you have read what you have read and know what you know.

You had probably heard about creative thinking before reading this. Chances are, though, that you probably did not see how it could be relative to you and your life. Now, though, you should see that it is very relevant and very useful in your life.

Adopting creative thinking is something that you may have to work at. You may need to try some techniques and practice in order to become a creative thinker. Your brain may not be predisposed to creative thinking, but that is okay. You can become a creative thinker.

All you have to do is learn to look beyond what is obvious. You have to think outside the boss. Do not jump on the band wagon. Try to find a different approach to problems. Try to think about things that may not even seem plausible. Take yourself to the limits with your ideas.

Do not be afraid to allow your brain to wander. Let your thoughts take over and make your logical brain take a back seat. Doing this can be described as just letting yourself daydream. Do not try to control your thoughts; let them flow.

Do not be worried about what others may think of your creative ideas. Stand behind them and be proud of them. If others are too objective of your ideas chances are they are just jealous they did not think of them first!

Use the advice and tips here to help you start to think creatively. Allow yourself to try out some of the thought experiments. Ask yourself a 'what if' question everyday. Keep up the work so you can really train your brain and make creative thinking second nature.

You hold the key to adopting creative thinking. It is all up to you. You have to expand your mind and you have to teach yourself to think freely. You have to make the commitment. You have to let go of the control that is holding you back from thinking creatively.

Creative thinking is something that can benefit you in many ways. You can change many things in your life by using creative thinking. You can advance at work and even learn to apply creative thinking in your everyday life.

You will find that creative thinking allows you to look at the world differently and to be able to grasp concepts that may have eluded you before. It is really beneficial to you. It will allow you to see everything around you in a different light. You may notice things that you overlooked before.

Sometimes we live life to fast, especially in this day and age. Being able to take the time to stop and notice all the little gems in life will be a good thing no matter what. Creative thinking can do that for you because you are slowing down your mind and pushing everything out but your ideas.

Do not be afraid of adopting creative thinking. Stand up for creative thinking and pass it on to people around you. Teach others how to be creative thinkers. It can really be catching. Do not be selfish and just let yourself keep creative thinking your secret. Tell others about it. Use Scott as an example. Let others benefit from what you know about creative thinking.

You can be a creative thinker. Just start letting your thoughts rule you instead of ruling your thoughts. Adopt creative thinking and you will begin to experience everything in a different way. You will see life in a different way and that alone can be extremely exciting and rewarding.

You are on your own now and only you can make the decision to adopt creative thinking in your life. Only you can be held responsible if you ignore all that you have learned. However, this is one last chance for you to read over what is written here and really take it to heart.

Creative thinking is a gift, a skill. Creative thinking is something you can live without, but why wouldn't you want to.Give it a try, at least and see how far it can take you. You will never know unless
you try. So, put creative thinking to work in your life starting today. Have a little fun training your mind to think creatively. Do not just walk away and never give creative thinking a thought.

The Art of Solving Problems

You likely use problem solving everyday. It is often taken for granted. People do not realize just how wonderful and important problem solving is. Most people do not even recognize it as a skill. In fact, most of the time problem solving is juts second nature.

Problem solving can actually be defined as an art. The art of problem solving is something that we learn at a very young age. It helps us through life and is something we could not live without. Being able to solve problems is a life skill. It is important and it should be taken seriously to get the best results from it.

Looking at problem solving as an art can help you to become more appreciative of it. You can begin to use problem solving to its full potential and really respect that problem solving is important. You just need to learn more about problem solving as a skill and an art.

The Importance of Problem Solving

Problem solving is a fixture in life. You have to be able to solve problems. Problems pop up everyday. Sometimes they are small and sometimes they are large. Sometimes solving a problem is a matter of life and death and other times it is merely a matter of keeping your sanity. Regardless of why you need problem solving, you can not deny that you need it.

If you are a parent, then problem solving is a skill you no doubt could not live without. Children are full of problems and as the parent it is up to you to help them find the solution. Sometimes you have to be creative because problems that come up can sometimes be quite difficult to solve without a little creative thinking.

The same can be said in business. Businesses have plenty of problems and it is up to the employees to find a way to solve those problems. Again, sometimes simple problem solving techniques just are not going to work because some problems require more problem solving skills.

You run into problems everyday, from flat tires to saving a failing product line. You are a problem solver and you probably do not even realize it. You should pay attention to your problem solving skills, though.

It is common for people to take problem solving for granted. We do it so much that it is not hard to believe that it becomes second nature. It is this familiarity with problem solving that leads up to take it for granted and to not be creative with our problem solving anymore.

If you think about how you solved problems when you were a child, chances are that you were much more creative then. Now you likely go straight to the tried and true methods instead of trying new things.

The problem with this, though, is that taking problem solving for granted can make you a lazy problem solver. You may no longer spend time trying to solve a problem but rather go to a tried and true solution. It may not be the best solution but since you are a lay problem solver you do not take the time to actual use your problem solving skills to try to come up with a better solution.

Problem solving can be an amazing process, but it is up to you to make it that way instead of just something you do because you have to. You have the ability to become a great problem solver, but you have to begin looking at it as an art.

Problem Solving from a Child's View

As mentioned, children solve problems much differently than adults. That is because children have less skill in problem solving and far less experience with problems and problem solving. The way children solve problems, though, can teach you a lot.

A child approaches a problem with an open mind. That is probably not something you do. You probably approach a problem with some preconceived notions about how it is all going to end. You probably come at it with a negative attitude and look at the problem as an annoyance. A child, on the other hand, looks at it as a challenge. They think of a problem as a great mystery and are excited about solving it.

You likely become frustrated when you can not fix the problem right away. A child, though, will become more excited. They will try different things until they find what works. They will experiment and they will just keep at it until they succeed. Adults are more likely to give p or just ask someone else to do it for them.

A child solves problems with wonder, amazement and persistence. Adults want problems to solve themselves because they do want to take the time to solve them properly.

The difference between how adults and children solve problems speaks volumes about how much we take problem solving for granted. Adults tend to be so worried about the time a problem will take to solve than actually being happy about succeeding at solving a problem.

If you can simply imply child like problem solving techniques you will find that solving problems becomes easier and more enjoyable. You will begin to be able to see problem solving as an art not an inconvenience.

Aspects of Problem Solving

The art of problem solving involves more than just jumping to the easiest solution. You have to really take time and analyze the problem. You have to come up with various solutions so you can find the perfect solution. You have to really make a conscious effort to solve a problem in a new way or the best way.

Here are some aspects of problem solving that you should start to use. You should take these aspects and apply them the next time you have a problem, no matter how big or small it is. You will then be able to understand the art of problem solving.

1 **Being flexible.** As mentioned, you have to go beyond your comfort zone. You have to avoid the immediate urge to go to the tried and true. You have to be flexible and willing to try something different. You will never know how great a solution may be if you do not try it.

2 **Take time to think.** You may need to step back and consider the situation before acting. You should brainstorm a little about the different ways you can solve this problem. Look at your options and stop before taking action.

3. **Ask questions.** Part of solving a problem is to create new questions to answer. You may think this is silly and compounding a problem, but really by asking questions you will be led to deeper solutions.

4. **Look at the problem in a different way.** Do not approach the problem as you normally would. Try thinking differently about it. Avoid your natural tendencies. This may be hard at first but once you get used to thinking differently it will become second nature.

5. **Think unconventionally.** Come up with solutions that make no sense. You might surprise yourself and actually run across an unconventional idea that is the perfect solution to your problem.

By using these ideas you can begin to start looking at problem solving in a whole new way. You will no longer just jump to the obvious conclusion, but rather be able to really find the perfect solution.

All it really involves is stepping back and taking some time. Not all problems must be solved right away. It is those problems that really let you put the art of problem solving to good use.

Skills for Problem Solving

Problem solving involves many different skills. The most important skills are outlined below.

1. **Creative thinking.** You have to be able to think in a creative manner and to se beyond the obvious if you ever want to be a good problem solver. You cannot just stick to the obvious because in most cases that will never get the problem solved. You have to be willing to think outside the box, brainstorm a little and come up with a unique solution. Creative thinking can make a person a perfect problem solver. Being able to think creatively allows a person to come up with solutions to problems that others may never even think about. A person is able to come up with good ideas that may not be so obvious. Creative thinking is something that can be a huge benefit to almost any profession because quick thinking is a great skill.

2. **Reasoning.** Reasoning has a place in problem solving, but it is important not to let your reasoning overtake your creativity. Reasoning comes I handy, though, because it will help you weed out the good ideas form the bad ones to come to the final solution.

3. **Objectivity.** You have to be object when approaching a problem. You can not have preconceived notions about how the situation will end or how you can fix the problem quickly. You have to come to a problem with an open mind and the ability to try different things to solve it.

4. **Positive attitude.** Your attitude can go a long way in your success as a problem solver. You have to be positive. If you approach a problem thinking that you will not be able to solve it then chances re that you will not be able to do it. You have to think positive and believe in yourself.

These skills will go a long way towards helping you be a good problem solver. The skills listed above are some of the major things you need in order to be able to solve problems in a constructive manner.

If you have these skills then you need to refine them. If you do not have these skills then you need to work on them. If you are committed to becoming a good problem solver then you need to have these skills to help you.

You can build upon these skills too to help you become an even better problem solver. There are also other skills not listed above that can assist you in being a good problem solver. You just need to identify what things you already know or can do that could possible be put to good use when you are solving problems.

Take inventory of your skills. You will find that many things you may not exactly see as a skill is actually a very nice asset to your problem solving skills. Go through your skills and see how each skill you have can in some way benefit your ability to solve problems.

Finding a Method of Problem Solving

Not everyone will solve problems in the same way. That is just part of what makes us each unique individuals. However, you can often learn from others and how they solve problems. They may use a technique that is new to you or something that really works and that you'd like to use. Watch how others solve problems and see what you can learn form them.

There are many methods of problem solving. You probably use one method and stick to it to solve every problem you encounter. This can be a bad thing. You should try out different methods because sometimes one method works better for a particular problem then another method.

There are three main ways people solve problems:

1. **Questions.** Some people solve problems by asking questions. They look at the problem and ask 'what if' – what if I tried this or what if this happens? Through questioning they are able to see the possible outcomes. This allows them to come up with the best solution that seems to be the one that will work to solve the problem.

2. **Develop a process.** For the more organized individual or the more complex problem it can sometimes help to develop a problem solving process. This usually involves analyzing the problem, proposing different solutions, testing the solutions and then finally, applying the chosen solution. It is a very structured way of solving a problem.

3. **Brainstorming.** For the more creative problem solver, there is the process of brainstorming. This involves just sitting down and coming up with numerous ways to solve the problem. Some ideas may be out there and that is fine. Using innovative thinking and being creative can help a person come up with an unconventional solution to a problem.

Being able to solve problems is a natural thing that we all are born with. It is actually how you approach problem solving that will help determine how good of a problem solver you are.

You should be willing to try different methods and different ways of problem solving. This will allow you to be able to come up with many options as a solution to your problem. You will then be more likely to come up with the perfect solution.

Putting the Art of Solving Problems to Use

Once you have developed a good understanding of problem solving that goes beyond the basic necessity for it, you can then truly start to recognize and grasp the idea of problem solving as an art.

You are able to start using problem solving in a different way. You can begin to become a master problem solver. People will start to see you as the solution person. They will come to you for advice and help when they have problems.

You will also be able to avoid problems in your life and solve them when they do come up. You will soon find that the art of problem solving is something you can not live without.

Being able to look at problem solving in a different way will help you to approach problems differently. You will not dread them when they pop up, but rather embrace them and start working on finding a solution.

Besides dealing with problems, problem solving will really help make your life much smoother. You will be able to handle adversity easier. In the long run you will start to feel better about yourself and be happier overall.

Problem solving is not just a skill, but an art. It can change your life for the better. Being able to solve problems quickly and efficiently is something that not everyone can do.

Not everyone can see a problem and take it as a challenge. Some people simply break down in the face of problems. These people have a hard time in life and business. You can get on top of the game with your ability to solve problems.

It all starts with being able to recognize problems and put the problem solving methods to good use. You have to remain calm and level headed so you can seek out the solution that works best.

Give up the Negative

One of the keys to becoming a good problem solver is to give up the negative. You have to approach problem solving in a positive way or you will never get anywhere.

Many times people approach a problem with their mind already made up that they will never solve it. If you think you cannot do something then chances are you will fail when you try. You have to think positively. You have to go at a problem thinking I can solve this, no problem.

A positive attitude is about keeping your mind open, which is important to problem solving, in general. When you approach a problem with a can do attitude you are able to stop yourself form getting frustrated easily. You are more open to letting your ideas flow and more likely to try out several solutions.

A positive attitude may just be the single hang up you have. Think about how you approach problems. Are you always going into the situation thinking you will never solve the problem? If so, then maybe simply by changing your attitude you can improve your problem solving skills.

Give it a try. The next time you approach a problem, think positively. Tell yourself you can do it, that you can solve the problem. Do not let yourself go to the negative.

A positive attitude is a major thing when it comes to problem solving. Do not forget that your attitude can be a huge influence. Keep it positive for the best results.

Problem Solving Exercises

There are many ways to practice your problem solving. You just have to take the time to practice. As with any skill the more you work at it the better you will become at it. You have to practice to be a good problem solver.

Here are some exercises you can do to help you become a better problem solver, open your mind and get yourself into the problem solving state of mind.

1 **Exercise 1:** Play games. Any type of game, whether it is a board game, card game or even a word search, will open your mind. It gets you thinking. It brings out the problem solving skills and it gets your mind in problem solving mode. Play games often so you can build up your mind and get it used to solving problems.

2 **Exercise 2:** Play with a child. Children are free thinking. They use their imagination all the time. They see the world around them as amazing and exciting. They are constantly exploring. They love to tackle problems. Spending some time with a child will allow you to see the world the way they do. You will be able to take away a little of their amazement and wonder that you can use in your problem solving.

3 **Exercise 3:** Experience something new. When you try something new you are earning new things, expanding your mind and opening yourself up to new problems that need solved. You will be able to practice your problem solving and learn something at the same time.

4 **Exercise 4:** Solve problems that already have a solution. Practice makes perfect so you need to practice your problem solving. The best way to do this is to take problems that

have already been solved. Figure out how the solution was found. How did you come up with the solution? By examining the solution to a problem you can learn a lot about the problem solving process. You will be able to take away from this exercise some key information that will help you to solve problems in the future.

These three exercises are not the only things you can do, but you should have a pretty good idea of what you need to do to help yourself start thinking like a master problem solver. It is all about opening your mind and practicing your problem solving methods.

An Example of Problem Solving at Work

The concept of how children solve problems verses how adults solve problems is one that you should fully understand. It is very important because we lose those good problem solving skills as we get older.

Part of the reason for this is that we become more logical. We no longer want to try to be creative. We want to go straight to what we are sure will work. We do not give anything else a try and if what we think will work turn out not to work, we get frustrated.

Another thing is we lose our sense of experimentation. We just do not want to take the time to try different ideas or even come up with different ideas. We get lazy.

As mentioned children do things much differently. Here is an illustrated example of how a child and adult would approach the same problem.

Situation: Bob and his son, Bob junior, are given a video game system to hook up to a television set. Bob is 28 and Junior is 8. Neither have directions and neither of them have set up a system like this before.

Bob: Bob's first instinct is to get out all the cords and pieces and lay them out nicely. He then examines each piece to see how everything fits together. He determines that there needs to be a cord running from the television to the game system and he picks up one that looks good. He then hooks up all the cords to the spots where they appear to go and turns on the system only to find that nothing happens. He unhooks everything and tries again and again. Eventually he gets frustrated and asks if the system is broken.

Junior: Junior dives right in just connecting cords. He ends up with the system hooked to the television, but nothing happens. He realizes he forgot to plug in the system and does so, but that doesn't make it show up on the television. Instead of unhooking everything he starts messing with the television. He end sup turning the channel and viola the system is working.

Bob was quick to give up and he missed the obvious – plugging the system in. Bob's first instinct was to make an excuse and say the system was broken. Junior kept at it and tried new things until he figured it out.

The difference in how they solved the problem is clear. Bob probably would have figured it out eventually, but Junior was the one to actually succeed. He never gave up and he was willing to experiment. Plus he did not miss the obvious because he was so focused on other things like his dad.

The way children solve problems is amazing. It is really something you can learn from. When you are solving problem strive to be more like Junior and less like Bob.

Summing It Up

Problem solving is an art because it takes a real creative mind to be a good problem solver. It involves creative thinking and it is something you can learn to do. As an art it should be held in high esteem. Problem solving needs to be taken seriously, but not too seriously.

As demonstrated adults tend to lose their problem solving skills. Adults are too quick to just want to get things done. They do not take the time to really think. Thinking is an important part of problem solving. Thinking involves not only looking at the obvious but also considering the not so obvious.

Children are master problem solvers because they are not afraid to try anything. Children will work and experiment and take the time to solve a problem. They do not care if people think they are weird for spending so much time to solve a problem. They are having fun trying to solve problems and they see it as a challenge or a game more then work.

Adults, on the other hand, just would rather give up then even put forth some effort. They see solving problems as just one more thing they have to do. It is work. There is nothing fun about it.

They can not see that problem solving can be something fun and exciting – it is just all about the way you approach it and look at it. That is why we have to go back to thinking about problems and approaching them in the same way we did as a child.

You have to approach problems with an attitude that is positive. You have to believe you can solve the problem and not immediately think about how hard it is going to be. You have to believe in your abilities. Self doubt can kill even the best problem solving efforts. If you never believe that you can solve a problem then you probably will never be able to solve the problem.

Your mind is very powerful. You have probably been told before that whatever you put your mind to you can accomplish. Well, the same is true for what you mind against. If you think that you can not do something then you will not be able to do it. It really is that simple. Your mind is that powerful. Mind over matter – that saying says it all.

You have to try different things and work towards a solution instead f just waiting for the solution to become clear. You have to work at problem solving, but at the same tie you have to be creative with your problem solving.

Problem solving is something we are born to do. Problems come in every shape and size. They can be small or they can be huge. You have to always be prepared because most often problems come unexpectedly. They will just appear and you have to deal with them.

You can not avoid problems, so it is only logical to become a good problem solver. A good problems solver is going to be an asset. They are someone good to have around. Make yourself that problem solver. Be the person everyone loves to have around. Be the person who can look at a complex situation and come up with a solution. Do not be the person that runs away and says I don't know or I can't do it.

There is no room for negative words when it comes to problem solving. Always remember that. Remember also, Bob and Junior. Be a junior, not a Bob. Don't give up or make excuses. Tackle problems and make the effort to solve them. Put your mind to it and you can be a great problem solver.

Put the art of problem solving to work in your life and you will be amazed at how well it works. Stop giving up and passing them onto others. Solve your problems and you will be glad you did.

www.ingramcontent.com/pod-product-compliance
Ingram Content Group UK Ltd.
Pitfield, Milton Keynes, MK11 3LW, UK
UKHW041919190726
13854UKWH00003B/1323

9 781329 333956